# WALLSEND
## THROUGH TIME

Ken Hutchinson

AMBERLEY PUBLISHING

This book is dedicated to my late mother

DOROTHY MARY HUTCHINSON

First published 2009

Amberley Publishing Plc
Cirencester Road, Chalford,
Stroud, Gloucestershire, GL6 8PE

www.amberley-books.com

Copyright © Ken Hutchinson, 2009

The right of Ken Hutchinson to be identified as the
Author of this work has been asserted in accordance with the
Copyrights, Designs and Patents Act 1988.

British Library Cataloguing in Publication Data.
A catalogue record for this book is available from the British Library.

ISBN 978 1 84868 320 4

Typesetting and Origination by Amberley Publishing.
Printed in Great Britain.

# Introduction

Wallsend has constantly changed over time and continues to do so. It started life as the Roman Fort of Segedunum in 126 AD and soon developed a vicus, or town, outside the fort walls to accommodate the soldiers' families, local businesses and the bathhouse. Over the next three centuries the fort and the town saw many changes.

When the Roman occupation ended in the fifth century the fort was eventually abandoned. The stones were used by the monks of Jarrow and Tynemouth as well as local farmers and the land reverted back to agriculture. A new township developed at Wallsend Green away from the riverside probably to avoid Danish or Viking raiders using the river. In the mid twelfth century Holy Cross church was built mid-way between the villages of Wallsend and Willington to serve the communities of farmers in the townships. From about the same time a small settlement grew up on the riverside around the local salt pans at Howdon Panns, later developing other industries including shipbuilding, rope making and whaling.

From the eighteenth century coal mining commenced in the area and colliery houses were built close to the many pit shafts. Waggonways were built to transport the coal to the River Tyne, where it could be loaded onto ships. Wallsend coal was world-famous for its quality but in 1835 the worst-ever mining disaster took place at Wallsend Colliery with the loss of 102 men and boys.

By the early part of the twentieth century shipbuilding and coal mining dominated the town as terraced streets were developed to house the expanding workforce.

Major employers were to dominate the town from this period up until the 1980s including Swan Hunter, North East Marine, Wallsend Slipway, Clelands, Cooksons, Haggies Ropeworks, Thermal Syndicate and the Rising Sun Colliery. Wallsend High Street also developed as the main shopping and entertainment area with pubs, music halls and, later, cinemas meeting local needs.

Following the First World War the style of housing changed in

Wallsend from terraced housing into suburban estates to house the rapidly expanding population of the town. Following the building of the Coast Road in the 1960s major housing estates were developed to the north including Battle Hill and Hadrian Park.

In more recent years some of the old housing and industrial areas have been cleared and redeveloped for new industries, housing and Segedunum Museum.

Apart from growing up and going to school in Wallsend I also spent the majority of my career working as a town planner for North Tyneside Council and was directly involved in the many changes that have happened to the town over recent years. As I always carried a camera with me I was fortunate to be able to photograph buildings before they were demolished as well as the erection of new buildings.

The area of Wallsend covered in this book relates to the boundary of the Borough of Wallsend as it existed between 1910 and 1974 including Willington, Howdon, Willington Quay and areas north of the Coast Road including Battle Hill and Rising Sun.

Many photos have been donated to collections by individuals, too numerous to mention separately, but who hopefully will be pleased to share their images with a wider audience.

I would like to apologise in advance for any mistakes in the book as the dates of some pictures have had to be estimated and some of the information used has not been double checked with original sources.

When looking through the images used in the book it is amazing how much Wallsend has changed over the last thirty years I wonder if it will change as much over the next thirty!

Ken Hutchinson
July 2009

## Holy Cross Church

Holy Cross church was built around 1150 to serve the villages of Wallsend and Willington and continued in use until 1797. The original Holy Cross church was neglected and fell into a ruinous state. Following a campaign, the church ruins were consolidated in 1909 and the present metal boundary fence was built around the area. The gravestones were removed and placed within the reduced churchyard. The photographs show the ruins shortly before restoration and in 2009.

### Esso Northumbria at Swan Hunters

Esso Northumbria is seen towering over Davis Street before its launch in 1969. It was the first of eight super tankers built at Swan Hunters in the 1960s and 1970s. The houses closest to the shipyard had to keep their lights on during daylight hours as the tankers would block out the daylight. The later picture was taken in May 2009 and shows the site of Segedunum Roman Fort with the reconstructed bath house standing on the site previously occupied by houses in Davis Street.

## Swans Bank

For decades all traffic on Hadrian Road and Buddle Street ground to a halt around 4 p.m. during the week, as crowds of workers climbed up Swans Bank leaving the afternoon shift, as seen here in the late 1980s. The later picture was taken on 17 June 2000 as Roman re-enactment soldiers prepared to march to the Metro station to escort dignitaries back to the official opening of the new Segedunum Museum.

## B Pit

The B Pit shaft of the famous Wallsend Colliery was sunk immediately to the north-west of the Roman fort, on what later became the corner of Buddle Street and Carville Road. It was never built upon and became a builder's yard, enclosed by hoardings, as seen in the 1960s with Carville Chapel behind. The view in 1997 shows the very well-preserved remains of the colliery workings that had industrial archaeologists descending on the site from all over the country.

### Parochial Hall Park Road

The building in the centre of the photograph, taken in the mid-1980s, was St Columba's parochial hall, which was linked to the Roman Catholic church in Carville Road. It was also used as an overflow classroom for St Columba's junior school during the 1950s and '60s. It was demolished and replaced by housing in the late 1980s. The later picture was taken during the Wallsend Festival parade in 2003 and features unusual cycles.

## Wallsend Mural

The new mural depicting the history of Wallsend is unveiled by the mayor of North Tyneside, Norman Hunter, in 1988. The mural was paid for by British Gas, and was painted by Doug Ewan, a local artist. It was fully weatherproof and the later photograph shows it in the background behind the former Wallsend Heritage Centre in June 2000, when the new Segedunum Museum was opened, following a display of marching by the Ermine Street Guard.

## Grammar School

In 2003 the impressive architecture of the former Wallsend Grammar School had changed little from the original building built as Wallsend Secondary School and Technical Institute in 1914. It became Wallsend Grammar School in 1944 and Burnside High School in 1969. The inset shows the building being demolished in 2004. The new Burnside Business & Enterprise College was built behind the former school.

## Stead Memorial Church

Revd William Stead was the minister of the Congregational church in Howdon from 1849 to 1883 and was the father of the famous journalist and peace campaigner William T. Stead. He was also very active in the local community. The church seen here in 1905 was erected in 1891 in Bewicke Road, Willington Quay. The church was demolished in the 1980s and replaced by housing for the elderly, known as Hanover Gardens.

## Municipal Buildings, Wallsend

This picture was taken shortly after the municipal buildings opened in 1908 and four years later the public baths were opened in 1912. Over time, the police court and fire station moved elsewhere. The public baths closed in 1989. A crowd of walkers have gathered outside the town hall in September 2008, about to take part in a local history walk linked to the town hall centenary celebrations led by Steve Boundey and David Harding from the Wallsend Local History Society, seen here third and fifth from the left in the picture.

## Wallsend Municipal Buildings Foundation Stone

On 19 June 1907 the foundation stone for the Wallsend Municipal Buildings was laid by alderman William Boyd who had been the first mayor of Wallsend in 1901. The picture is taken looking north with Charlotte Street in the background and every dignitary in the town has been invited and has dressed for the occasion. In the view from 2009 the shop opposite has survived, but the terraced housing in Charlotte Street has been replaced by more modern housing and a garage workshop has also been built.

## Coach Open Corner Howdon on Tyne

The shop in the foreground is at the eastern end of Willington Quay and is situated in Church Street. Coach Open was the short curved street that linked Church Street with Stephenson Street to the south, immediately beyond the shop. The trams travelled up Coach Open on their way to North Shields. The later photograph, taken in April 2009, shows Coach Open from the south, with the fish sculpture in the foreground and the Tyne Tunnel Control Office in the background.

## St Luke's Church Hall

In 1908 St Luke's church hall was built at the rear St Luke's church on Frank Street. It served the church congregation and other local groups for 100 years, including, for a short time, Wallsend Local History Society. The concrete structure was showing its age when the decision was taken to demolish it. A block of flats and a new church hall, utilising part of the existing church, was approved to be built on the site. The later picture shows the flats being constructed in May 2009.

## Burn Closes Bridge

Burn Closes Bridge, seen here around 1923, was built in 1914. This uniquely designed ferroconcrete bridge was built by G. Wier Builders and later became a listed building. Unfortunately, over time, the bridge developed major structural problems and the bridge was demolished in late 2008. A pedestrian bridge was erected while the new bridge was built. The new bridge opened in March 2009 and is seen here after the pedestrian bridge was dismantled.

## Burn Closes Bridge Construction

The first picture, taken from the north in June 2008, shows the original Burn Closes Bridge, prior to its demolition, with the temporary footpath alongside it. The later picture, taken in late 2008, shows the new bridge under construction from the south. The new bridge cost £4.6 million and was opened on 26 March 2009 by Mr Geoff Hoon, Secretary of State for Transport assisted by the newly elected North Tyneside Young Mayor, Olamide Akinropo, a pupil at the nearby school.

## Our Lady and St Columba Roman Catholic Church

A new church was erected in 1904 in Carville Road. It was built close to the Roman Catholic school built in 1876. The church dedicated to Our Lady and St Columba was constructed in temporary materials and was locally known as the 'Tin Church' or 'Cathedral'. It is seen here in 1920. The present church of the same name was built in 1957. St Columba's junior school was partly demolished and converted into a church hall with a car park, following the building of a new school in Station Road.

Council Chambers. Willington Quay. (No. 105)

## Council Chambers Willington Quay

Before 1910, Willington Quay was a separate urban district council serving the townships of Howdon and Willington Quay. It was established in 1894 and ran its own affairs. The council chambers were situated on the south side of Bewicke Street on the corner of Carlyle Street above shop units built in 1891. These units were known locally as 'The Central' Co-op store, and were severely damaged by fire in 1959 and subsequently demolished. They were later to be replaced by housing.

## Allen Memorial Church

The Allen Memorial was built in 1904 and is seen here not long after its completion, and before the houses on North Road were built immediately in front. The buildings to the right of the church in the distance are the White House and adjoining farm buildings on the south side of Wallsend Green. The 2009 image shows that the church has now lost its steeple and the housing in North Road has been built. It also shows a recent block of flats, built in 2004.

Isolation Hospital, Wallsend,

### Isolation Hospital

The Isolation Hospital, referred to as the Infectious Diseases Hospital, is seen here in 1919. It was originally built in the 1890s in open fields adjoining Wallsend Dene. Later renamed Hadrian Hospital, it was closed in 1986 and was converted into a rest home known as Greenacres. This was then closed and was demolished to be replaced by the present Kings Vale housing development around 2000, seen here behind the ambulance station built in the 1980s.

ST AIDAN'S CHURCH, WILLINGTON QUAY.

## St Aidan's Church Willington Quay

St Aidan's church was opened in 1907 on the south side of the site, in front of the presbytery and the earlier chapel that were built in 1876. They can be seen behind the new church. The original school lay to the north of the chapel and was built about the same time. The church was considerably altered over time, including the erection of a major extension on its south side to form a new entrance. The church survived for 100 years before being demolished, along with the presbytery, after the later view was taken in July 2006.

## Duffy Memorial Ceremony

This carefully composed picture taken in Wallsend Park with the Allen Memorial in the background was printed on two postcards. As many people in the photograph appear to be dignitaries linked with Wallsend Borough Council, and as the now demolished Duffy Memorial Fountain was erected close to where the photograph was taken, the picture may well date from when the fountain was opened in 1912. Joseph Duffy was a former mayor of Wallsend who died in 1910 during his year in office.

## Police Station Wallsend

The police station was built in Alexandra Street in 1915 to replace the old police station on the corner of the Avenue and High Street West. This photograph must have been taken shortly after this, from the style of the clothes worn by the children. It also shows open land in the foreground, later to be converted into allotments that are still there today. The recent image, taken in 2009, shows little change, apart from the loss of the railings and a remodelled new entrance with ramps.

### Addison Potter Schools Willington Quay

The schools were named after the prominent industrialist and local politician Addison Potter who was the first chairman of the Willington Quay Local Board in 1863 as well as chairman of the school and health boards. He was the owner of a firebrick works which later developed into a cement works. The infant school, seen here in the early 1900s, was built on a site adjoining Clavering Street in 1887 and later extended. The site is now occupied by Eldon Court residential home and other housing.

## Richardson Dees School

Robert Richardson Dees was a solicitor who lived in Wallsend Hall from 1856 to 1908, when he died aged ninety-five. He donated the land at the former colliery C Pit site to the council in 1897 to form a public park which was named after him. When this school was built in 1902 it was also named after him. This postcard view was postmarked 1912. The later view was taken in 2009 and shows how the front of the school was altered considerably in the mid-1980s.

The Lake, Wallsend Park.

## The Lake, Wallsend Park

The lake in Wallsend Park was formed as part of the overall works to create a public park on the site of wasteland previously forming part of the redundant colliery. The lake was formed where two water courses met. The wooded steep-sided valleys still provide a wildlife haven, and the island built in the lake still provides a shelter for ducks and other wildlife. The first image, on a postcard postmarked 1928, shows swans and ducks entertaining the children.

## War Memorial Wallsend

The obelisk is a rare design for a war memorial in the North East. This memorial in Archer Street was erected following the First World War in the early 1920s. It is made from granite and supports a bronze winged figure of Peace standing on a polished granite sphere (see inset). The earlier photograph, taken soon after the memorial was erected, shows that the surrounding area had been landscaped using large rocks and mounds of earth but these have now been removed in favour of grass and planted beds.

## Church Bank

This postcard image, postmarked 1912, shows Church Bank close to the entrance of the Church Bank Cemetery. The original fencing is still in position around the cemetery. Horses and carts and trams on the road leading to and from Rosehill Bank are visible in the picture. This picture was taken before the new Rose Inn was built in 1913 and the old Rose Inn is hidden from view behind trees just above the second tram. The later picture taken in 2009 shows that the railings have been removed.

## Church Bank from Rosehill

This picture was taken in about 1915, as the secondary school, built in 1914, can be seen in the background. The open-top tram in the foreground has a large number of people taking advantage of the good weather by sitting on the top deck. Several houses can be seen in the foreground and on the bank side, all of which have disappeared by the 1980s. The view below was taken before 1914 as the secondary school has not been completed.

NEPTUNE ROAD WALLSEND. (614).

### Neptune Road, Wallsend

This image was taken in about 1915, looking east along Neptune Road and shows buildings on both sides of the road, with the main offices of the Gas Board, later Thermal Syndicate and after that The Carers' Centre, immediately on the right. On the left, shops and housing front onto the main road linking Walker to Wallsend. The main tram works were located behind the Thermal Syndicate offices. All the roadside buildings on the north side of the road were cleared away in the 1970s and replaced by landscaping.

Hood Haggies Works, Willington Quay. (No. 106)

## Hood Haggies Works, Willington Quay

Rope works were established on this site in 1789 by William Chaplin and, in 1840, Robert Hood Haggie bought the business and ran it in his name. In 1873 there was a major fire at the works that destroyed most of the buildings and almost burnt down Willington Viaduct, which at the time was being converted from timber to iron construction. Bridon Fibres now operates from the site and all the buildings below and to the west of the viaduct have now been demolished.

## Willington Mill

Willington Mill was erected around 1750 on a bend in Willington Gut and was originally known as Proctor's Mill, after the original owner who built a large house beside it. The photograph was taken in 1893 and shows the seven-storey mill in the foreground with Proctor's house behind it. All that remains of the mill complex is Willington Mill which has been reduced to four storeys and now has a curved roof. Willington Mill is famous for its ghost, sometimes referred to as 'Kitty'.

## The Ferry Landing, Wallsend

Wallsend Ferry Landing was situated at the end of Benton Way. The Hebburn to Wallsend ferry opened in 1904 and closed in 1986 as shipbuilding work had declined on the river. The first picture is taken from the ferry landing looking back over Swan Hunters Shipyard in 1986 with the *Sir Galahad* under construction. The later picture was taken in Hebburn in 2001 at the point where the ferry landing used to be in Ellison Street.

## Wallsend Golf Course 1905

The first Wallsend Golf Course was opened in 1905 to the north of Tynemouth Road and to the east of Churchill Street in Howdon. H. Crawford Smith MP is seen driving the first ball on 3 June of that year. In the background are Bewicke Schools and the caretaker's house. The golf club was displaced from the site in 1941 by the army. The Bewicke schools were demolished in the mid-1980s to be replaced by the Tynemouth Road Medical Centre and sheltered housing.

## Bewicke School

The Bewicke school was built fronting onto Tynemouth Road in 1875, together with a house for the headteacher and caretaker. It was built in the Scottish Baronial style similar to the Buddle school in Wallsend and was named after the Bewicke Family from Newcastle who owned the land. The school was demolished in the mid-1980s and the site was redeveloped soon afterwards.

## O'Hare and Bowman

Situated in open fields on the Old Coast Road, O'Hare and Bowman Ltd was one of the first garden centres in the area. It originated as a market garden, and then started to sell plants and produce to the public. In the early 1980s the Co-op developed the site and built their first hypermarket on the adjoining site together with a purpose built garden centre for O'Hare and Bowman Ltd. The site was later taken over by Asda.

## St Peter's Court

St Peter's School was the first purpose-built school in Wallsend and opened in 1833 on Church Bank. The original building was built in stone and a later extension, constructed about 1930 was built in brick and extended the school further down the hill. The photograph taken in 1994 shows the brick-built extension in the foreground with the original school building beyond. At that time the school had closed. St Peter's Court was built on the site in 1996.

### Battle Hill House

Battle Hill House was one of the few original buildings on the Battle Hill Estate. It was built for the owners of the local colliery and used as an office for the Bewicke Coal Company and in later years it was used as a nursery and as offices for community organisations. It was demolished in 1997. The original walls remain with an old sign seen behind the fireman. Treetops housing development was built in the late 1990s.

## Buddle Street

Buddle Street in the 1960s before demolition works started, exposing the Roman fort of Segedunum. The Swan Hunters Institute Building is seen behind the clock at the top of Swans Bank and the large building behind it is Simpsons Hotel a local landmark until it was demolished in the late 1980s. Rows of houses led off Buddle Street to the north and south to house local workers. Ermine Street Guard march from Segedunum Fort on the day the museum opened on 17 June 2000.

## Buddle Street Excavation

In 1976 excavations of Segedunum Roman Fort were in full swing on the north side of Buddle Street opposite Simpsons Hotel. Wallsend Local History Society had an enthusiastic band of volunteer helpers who also provided refreshments (see inset). Former Chairman Harry Domoney is seen here second from the right standing on the foundations of a Roman barrack block. The above view, taken in 2008, shows how the remains of the buildings found during the excavations have now been laid out within Segedunum Roman Fort.

## Segedunum Excavation

Wallsend fort is the most excavated fort on Hadrian's Wall. In 1998 Dr Nick Hodgson is standing on the site of the hospital building explaining to visitors how the Romans may have used the only double seated toilet to be found on Hadrian's Wall. In the background workers are busy excavating. The later picture was taken on 17 June 2000 at the opening of the new Segedunum Museum and shows Bill Griffiths the curator of the museum.

### Segedunum Guided Tour 1987

Wallsend Heritage Centre, which stood opposite the present museum, was opened in 1986 and a number of volunteers were enlisted and trained to act as guides to the Roman fort. The author was one of the original guides and is seen here in 1987 with the Swan Hunter Canteen in the background. The lady in the foreground is the author's mother Dorothy Hutchinson and, to her left, is Beatrice Clark. The Ermine Street Guard re-enactment group are seen giving a demonstration in front of the tower of the new Segedunum Museum in 2001.

## Forum Clock

When Wallsend Forum Square was built in the mid-1960s the centrepiece of the development was the typical 1960s style iconic square tower clock with its brightly coloured mosaic style pattern. These views are from the early 1980s. The clock was removed when the Forum was redeveloped in the mid-1990s. The image below was taken in 2001 during the Wallsend Festival when King Kong entertained the crowds beside the plinth of the former clock.

## Holystone Hospital & Rising Sun Centre

Holystone Hospital, originally called Scaffold Hill Hospital, was built as an Isolation Hospital for Infectious Diseases by Earsdon Local Health Board around 1900. It got its original name from the grandstand (otherwise known as a scaffold) that existed on the site when the area had been used as a horse-racing track on Killingworth Moor. It is seen in 1986 shortly after the hospital closed. Today the buildings have been converted into the Rising Sun Countryside Centre.

## Western Schools

Western Schools were built on the site at West Street between Forrest Road and Rutland Road in 1910. The site had both infant and junior schools as well as playing fields on Rutland Road. The present new school was built in 2003 north of the old site (see inset). The old school buildings, seen from Rutland Road in 2004, were demolished shortly afterwards. The later picture, taken in 2009, shows the housing development that replaced the school.

### Fourteen Storey Flats

The blocks of flats erected at Willington Square in the 1970s were locally known as the fourteen storey flats. They dominated the skyline close to the Coast Road and were featured in the 1970's film *The Likely Lads*. The early image, taken in 1986, shows a side view of a tower block. The later picture, taken in 2009, shows how the site was redeveloped in the 1990s for low-rise housing.

## The *Atlantic Conveyor*

The *Atlantic Conveyor* was under construction in Swan Hunters shipyard in 1985 as the land in the foreground was undergoing a transformation, following excavations, to lay it out as open space with the outline of the Roman Fort displayed. In 2008 the cranes that dominated the skyline of Wallsend can be seen in the process of being demolished before being shipped off to India.

### RFA *Sir Galahad*

RFA *Sir Galahad* is seen here on the day of its launch in December 1986. This ship replaced a ship of the same name lost in the Falklands War of 1982. Swan Hunters shipyard was famous for building ships for the Royal Navy including the aircraft carriers HMS *Illustrious* and HMS *Ark Royal*. They continued building ships until 2005. In 2008 a number of cranes are seen loaded onto the dry dock awaiting transportation to India.

### The Stadium, Wallsend Green

The Stadium dominated the south side of Wallsend Green from 1910 till 1986 and it is seen here from North View. It was considered to be a major eyesore in Wallsend Green Conservation Area. In the late 1980s executive housing, called White House Mews, was built on the site and is seen here in 2009. The Villa is the large house to the east.

## Battle Hill Flats

In the 1970s there was great demand for housing in Wallsend and the Battle Hill Estate was developed north of the Coast Road. The estate was developed for both private and public housing and also included a new shopping centre and community facilities. The four-storey blocks of flats are seen here in 2008, just before they were demolished, to make way for the new shopping and community development seen under construction in May 2009.

## Battle Hill Shopping Centre

A new shopping centre was built for the new Battle Hill Estate in the 1970s including a local pub, club, library, medical centre and other community buildings. This view of Battle Hill Shopping Centre was taken in July 2006 looking towards the Emperor Hadrian pub (seen also in the inset). The later picture, taken in May 2009, shows the new shopping centre under construction on the south side of Battle Hill Drive.

## Monitor Engineering

Monitor Engineering was a long-established business in Wallsend that had a factory at the top of Kings Road. The 1960s-style office block was very dominant when viewed from the Coast Road, providing a contrast with the original red-brick factory buildings (seen in the inset). The earlier views date from July 2006 and the later view is after the new housing has been built in 2009.

## Wallsend Boys' Club

The Wallsend Boys' Club building in Station Road has not changed much in appearance since it was built in the 1960s. The club is famous for producing stars such as Alan Shearer, Michael Carrick, Peter Beardsley, Lee Clark and Steve Watson, to name but a few. The above picture shows the new Wallsend Boys' Club under construction in May 2009, with its own football pitches, beside the golf course.

## The North East Marine Crane

The NEM crane was the first electric cantilever crane on the north-east coast. It was 154ft tall and could lift 150 tons. The crane became a listed building but was demolished in 1995 after the site had been taken over for the construction of oil rig platforms. It is seen in 1985, shortly after North East Marine had closed. The later image was taken in 2009 from the Hadrian Road Metro Station, and shows that the former NEM canteen has been converted into the Hadrian Lodge Hotel.

## Northumberland Arms

At one time this site on the corner of Ravensworth Street and Tynemouth Road was occupied by the Kettle Inn on the east side and the Northumberland Arms on the west. The Northumberland Arms was rebuilt in the early 1990s and is shown here in October 2007 before demolition. The Kettle Inn was demolished and replaced by advertising hoardings mid-way through the 1900s.

## Howdon Library

Howdon Library was opened in 1959 on Churchill Street to serve the rapidly expanding population in the local area, as new housing estates were developed to the north of Tynemouth Road and east of Churchill Street. The library continued to provide books and CDs until January 2009 when this picture was taken shortly before it was demolished. The picture taken in May 2009 shows the site being redeveloped to provide a joint library and community facility.

## Old Police Station

The original Wallsend Police Station is seen here on the corner of The Avenue, High Street West and Portugal Place. It was built in the late 1800s with three cells and an exercise yard as well as police houses. The rear yard was shared with the officers of the first Wallsend Fire Brigade and access was gained through an archway from The Avenue, where a shopfront can be seen on the photograph taken in 1986. The residential home was built on the site in 1990.

## The Duke of York

This view of the Duke of York public house on High Street West was taken in 1986. This was before the new housing was erected between the pub and West Street, on what used to be a car park and, before that, air raid shelters and a builder's yard. The Duke of York was built about 1900 and was vacant when the later picture was taken in 2009.

## Wallsend Technical School

Wallsend Technical School was situated at the top of Boyd Road and shared a large site with Wallsend Grammar School and Central School. The 'Tec' provided opportunities for technical learning. The buildings in the foreground with the large glass windows were the metalwork shops, with anvils and forges. This view was taken in 2003 when the buildings formed part of Burnside High School. The new Burnside Business and Enterprise College can be seen in the background of the later picture, taken in 2009.

## DHSS Offices, The Green

The Department of Social Security Office occupied a prime site overlooking The Green Conservation Area to the west of the former stadium. The government building complex extended back to North View. In 1994, the DHSS offices are shown after the new houses at White House Mews had been constructed. The offices were demolished after 1997 and replaced by more housing, known as Hunters Court, as seen in the later view taken in 2009.

## The Ship in the Hole

The Ship in the Hole was one of the two pubs situated in Gainers Terrace, a small terraced street that ran below the old Riverside Railway and close to Swan Hunters shipyard. The other pub was the Dock Hotel, seen in the background in 1985, shortly before it was demolished. Also in the background are the offices of Wallsend Dry Docks and Ship Repair Yard. Only the Ship Inn, having reverted back to its original name, was in existence at the time of the later picture.

### Wallsend Town Hall

The early image dates from around 1912, from the style of dress, and clearly shows that the town hall buildings were surrounded by ornate railings before the war. The building celebrated its centenary in 2008 and has changed little externally.

## Killingworth Waggonway Bridge

In the background a farmer is seen leading his cows past the Killingworth Waggonway with the old Wallsend pumps in the foreground. The bridge served Killingworth Colliery, transporting coal to the River Tyne and it was demolished after 1940. The Wallsend pumps provided water for residents of Wallsend village centred on Wallsend Green; they were removed some time after 1914. The site of the bridge is now obscured by trees, as seen from the view taken from Holy Cross steps.

## Wallsend Dene

In this scene, looking north towards Wallsend Dene, cows are being led towards Crow Bank on the way to one of the farms on Wallsend Village Green. On the hill to the right, behind the tree, are the ruins of Holy Cross church. Only the base of the Wallsend pumps has survived and can be seen in the centre of the later image.

## St Mary's Church Willington Village

St Mary's church is seen here from the east, viewed from Willington Stables that can be seen on the right-hand side of the picture. Willington Stables stood to the north of the present Perth Gardens and east of Churchill Street; it was still quite a large settlement when the 1918 Ordnance Survey Map was published. The later image is taken from Churchill Street looking east.

## The Bridge in Hall Grounds

The Hall Grounds are now a public park but was once laid out as pleasure grounds connected to the largest house on Wallsend Green, Wallsend Hall. The ornamental bridge, seen in the early 1900s, was one of many features in the pleasure grounds that also included a grotto and vinery. Sir George Hunter gave both the hall and its grounds to Wallsend Corporation in 1916. The later view was taken in 1986 and Wallsend Hall is seen in the inset.

## Wallsend Burn and Viaduct

Wallsend Burn is seen meandering through the Burn Closes with the Willington Viaduct in the background. The picture was taken before 1913 because the new Rose Inn has not yet been built and it was also before improvement works took place to realign the course of Wallsend Burn. The later picture shows a recent close-up of the viaduct.

## St Columba's School 1930

Bishop Thorman is seen laying the foundation stone for St Columba's school on Hedley Street on 21 June 1930. The building included both a junior school on the ground floor and a secondary modern above and was demolished in 1974 to make way for housing. The building featured in the later picture is now St Columba's church hall but was previously used as an infant school.

## Wallsend Views

Two postcards of Wallsend featuring different local views. The black and white card dates from the 1930s and shows the recently built St Columba's school and new housing on Kings Road. The coloured card dates from 1915 and is of Wallsend Park, including a view of the re-erected Roman wall, that was excavated from Swan Hunters shipyard, in 1902, as well as highlighting the Slipway and NEM cranes.

### Elm Terrace, The Village

Elm Terrace has changed little despite the pictures being taken about 100 years apart. The trees have certainly grown a lot in the intervening years on the village green and they now obliterate Hawthorn Villas to the west of Elm Terrace. Hawthorn Villas dates from 1897 and Elm Terrace from the early 1870s.

## Wallsend Church and Stocks

Wallsend church or St Peter's is seen in the 1920s and again in 2009 in its bicentennial year. Sabbath breaking in Wallsend must have been a problem in the nineteenth century as stocks were installed in the church grounds in 1816 to punish those who missed the Sunday services. The inset photo shows the stocks positioned originally beside the main gate and they have since been moved to beside the church entrance.

## Wallsend Park Bowling Green

The bowling green in Wallsend Park is seen about 1910 looking north with views across rolling fields and a few isolated buildings. Today the trees have grown to mask any view to the north but the bowling greens are still popular with residents of Wallsend.

## The Park and Children

This view of Wallsend Park was taken early in the 1900s from the dress of the children who are all taking a keen interest in what the photographer is doing. The camera is pointing north and the children in the distance are at the end of the park that now adjoins Princes Road. This long view is no longer possible in the summer as the trees now obscure the view, as seen in a view across the bowling greens, with a group of bowlers in the background.

## The Park, Wallsend

Families enjoy lakeside walks in Richardson Dees Park in this photograph taken around 1910. The houses on Kings Road are now hidden by trees.

## Lake and Bridge in Richardson Dees Park

Workmen are seen putting the finishing touches to the landscaping around the lake in Richardson Dees Park in the early part of the 1900s. The landscaping has proved very successful and it is now impossible to capture the same view through the trees in the summer.

Allen Memorial Church, Wallsend.  ( No. 112 )

## Allen Memorial Church from The Green

Allen Memorial Church is seen here from The Green, with its original spire, around 1915. The Buddle school is in the background. The spire has now been removed from the church and the trees now dominate the boundary of the park. The old caretaker's house at the Buddle school has been converted into part of the Surestart children's complex, which has also incorporated a former handball wall into the new buildings.

## Burn Closes Bridge and Bus

Burn Closes Bridge is seen here from the east with a double-decker bus on top heading towards Wallsend in the 1950s. Buses were one of the first vehicles to be banned from using the bridge when it started to suffer from structural problems in the 1990s and this proved very inconvenient to residents of Holy Cross housing estates. The bridge was replaced in 2009 with the present-day bridge shown below with a single-decker bus crossing it.

## High Street West and the Black Bull

The Black Bull Hotel features prominently in this picture of High Street West taken in the 1920s. The view looks west towards the boundary with Newcastle just out of the picture. The buildings to the west of the Black Bull were demolished in the late 1930s to make way for the Ritz Cinema, now the Mecca Bingo Hall and the Black Bull is now 'The Klub'.

## High Street, Wallsend 1902

This postcard view, postmarked 1902, was taken on Wallsend High Street West looking east towards the rear of Wallsend Café on the right and the spire of the Brunswick Methodist church on the left. The horse and cart is parked up outside the shops that were later demolished to make way for the Forum Shopping Centre. The road off to the right is Atkinson Street. The later image was taken in 2009.

## High Street East

Central Buildings, known as the 'Boots' buildings, are seen on the left, on the corner of Station Road and High Street East and dominate this photograph that was taken shortly after they were built in 1910. In the days before traffic lights on the junction, policemen were often seen directing traffic on the busiest junction in Wallsend. The Wallsend Festival in 2004 closed the High Street to traffic to make way for vintage vehicles, funfair rides and other activities outside the busy Woolworth's store.

## High Street

This view, taken about 1912 from High Street East, is looking at a tram in High Street West that is about to cross Station Road. The old buildings on the south-east corner of Station Road were cleared by 1916 and this site was later occupied by Woolworths. Boots occupied the opposite corner for many years before moving into the Forum Shopping Centre, which was developed in the mid-1960s and can be seen on the later picture beyond the car.

HIGH STREET, WALLSEND-ON-TYNE    L 81

### High Street East

The junction of Station Road and High Street East is seen here in the 1950s. Boots occupies the site on the north-east side and Burtons the diagonally opposite site just beyond the Midland Bank, on the right-hand side of the picture. The later view shows that Brunswick Methodist church with its impressive spire has been demolished and replaced by flats.

## Rosehill, Wallsend

Rosehill Terrace dominates the skyline on the north side of Rosehill Bank. Just beyond the tram travelling down Church Bank, the new Rose Inn can be seen and the picture must be dated after 1914, as that was the date that the pub was built. The recent picture shows new housing in the place of Rosehill Terrace, but in the intervening period this was the site of blocks of flats from the 1970s to the 1980s.

## Burn Closes and Old Wooden Bridge

Wallsend Burn is seen flowing through the Burn Closes in the 1920s with the old wooden Killingworth Waggonway Bridge in the background. This was before improvement works were undertaken to straighten the course of the burn as seen on the later picture. The bridge was demolished after 1940.

Burn Closes, Wallsend.    79747. JK.

## Burn Closes and Bridge

This picture was taken shortly after the Burn Closes Bridge was completed in 1914 and the construction site appears to be fenced off. The picture is taken looking east towards Rosehill with Rosehill Terrace and other housing visible through the arches of the bridge. The later picture shows the recently completed new Burn Bridge in 2009.

## St Andrew's Mission, Bigges Main

St Andrew's mission church, seen here in 1909, was in the centre of the former mining village of Bigges Main. The village occupied the site of the Wallsend Golf Course and the former Wallsend Sports Centre, seen in the later view, at Rheydt Avenue, south of the Coast Road. On the 1916 Ordnance Survey Map, Bigges Main was still a large village with its own school and pub. The old colliery rows were gradually demolished and the last building, the Masons Arms, was demolished in the late 1960s.

## Park Road Looking North

In 1910 this is what Park Road looked like, with the recently opened Borough Theatre dominating the street scene on the east side and a bank on the west side. The Borough Theatre was still in place in 2009, although it had been derelict for some time and its future is uncertain. A bank operated from the other corner until the 1980s before changing into retail use.

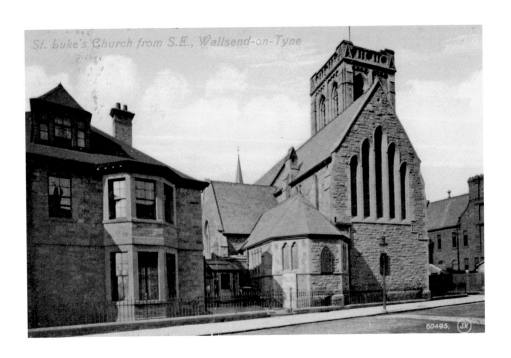

## St Luke's Church

The postcard of St Luke's church dates from about 1909 before the shops were built on the corner of Frank Street and Station Road and the Memorial Hall on Frank Street. This view has changed very little apart from the loss of the metal railings around the site.

## Wallsend Harriers

Wallsend Harriers appear to have had a successful year from the trophies on display in this photograph dated 1922. Wallsend Harriers continue to be an active club as seen in the photograph taken in 1998 when a group of runners were photographed passing Segedunum Roman Fort as works were underway on the new museum.

## Old Rose Inn

The Old Rose Inn was a coaching inn on the Newcastle to North Shields Turnpike Road and it was showing its age when it was demolished in 1913 following the opening of the New Rose Inn. The Old Rose Inn is seen in the distance in the centre of the picture between Rosehill Terrace above and Haggies ropeworks below. The New Rose Inn was built immediately to the west and slightly downhill from the Old Rose Inn and will soon be celebrating its own centenary.

## Wallsend Scout Troop

This postcard was found in the Wallsend Local History collection and notes on the back indicate that it is a picture of the 1st Wallsend Scout Troop taken in about 1918. The later picture was taken at the Wallsend Festival Parade in 2003 and shows the girls and boys of the Sea Cadets carrying a model ship.

A 84971 J.V.      WALLSEND SLIPWAY FROM THE AIR

### An Aerial View of Wallsend Slipway

This postcard gives a view of Wallsend Slipway from the air and dates from around 1910. The company supplied marine engines for vessels built at Swan Hunters and other yards on The Tyne and used the massive hammerhead crane to lift the engines into the ships. The later picture shows the Wallsend Slipway crane shortly before demolition in 1987.

## Wallsend Slipway

The Wallsend Slipway crane is seen in the first picture in 1986 before it was demolished. Rows of pleasure craft await the next high tide in the second picture at the Willington Gut Marina in 2009.

# Acknowledgements

This book has been written on behalf of Wallsend Local History Society and all proceeds from the royalties will be shared between the Society and St Oswald's Hospice in Newcastle.

The Society was established in 1973 and meets in the Wallsend Memorial Hall, Station Road at 7 p.m. every second Monday in the month.

I wish to record my special thanks to all who have helped me in the past and especially to those recently active on the committee: Edmund Hall, Dorothy Hall, Steve Boundey, Bill Baxter, David Harding, John Stephenson, Don Price, Vera Pace, Brian Robson, Fiona Jackson, Joyce Smith, and Barry Martin. I have used a number of photographs from the Society's collection as well as some from the private collections of Beatrice Clark, Marjory Hall and Doris Thurlbeck.

I would also like to thank North Tyneside Libraries for the use of a number of old photographs from their excellent Local Studies collection. Special thanks are due to their dedicated and helpful staff in particular Eric Hollerton, Alan Hildrew and Diane Leggett. I would like to take this opportunity to encourage anyone who has any old photographs of buildings or scenes in Wallsend to make them available to the Local Studies Library in North Shields Central Library or to Wallsend Local History Society.

I would also like to thank North Tyneside Council for allowing me to use a number of photographs taken over time by the planning team. Special thanks also go to all my previous work colleagues for their help and encouragement over the years.

My thanks are also due to the Tyne and Wear Museum Service and especially the staff at Segedunum Roman Fort, Baths and Museum and the Committee of Friends of Segedunum.

Finally, I would like to thank my wife Pauline for proof-reading the text and her encouragement and also my sons Peter and David for putting up with being dragged all around the back streets of Wallsend when they were young, while I took photos.